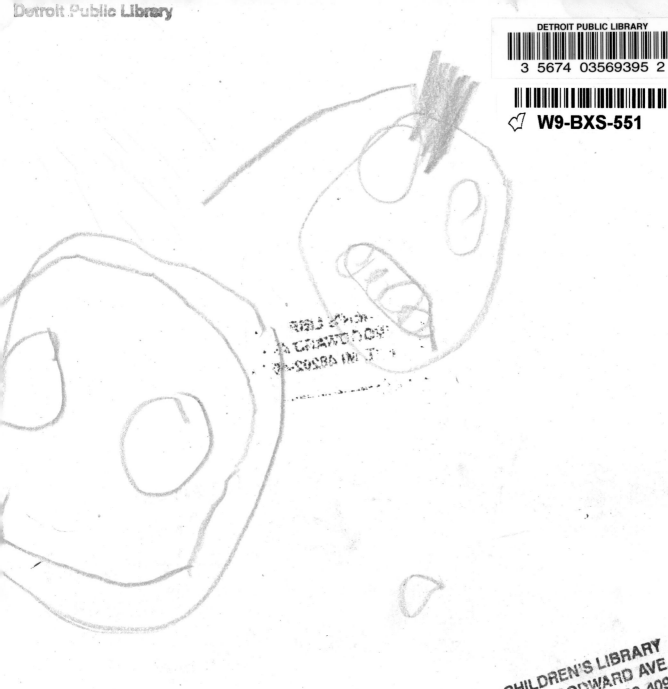

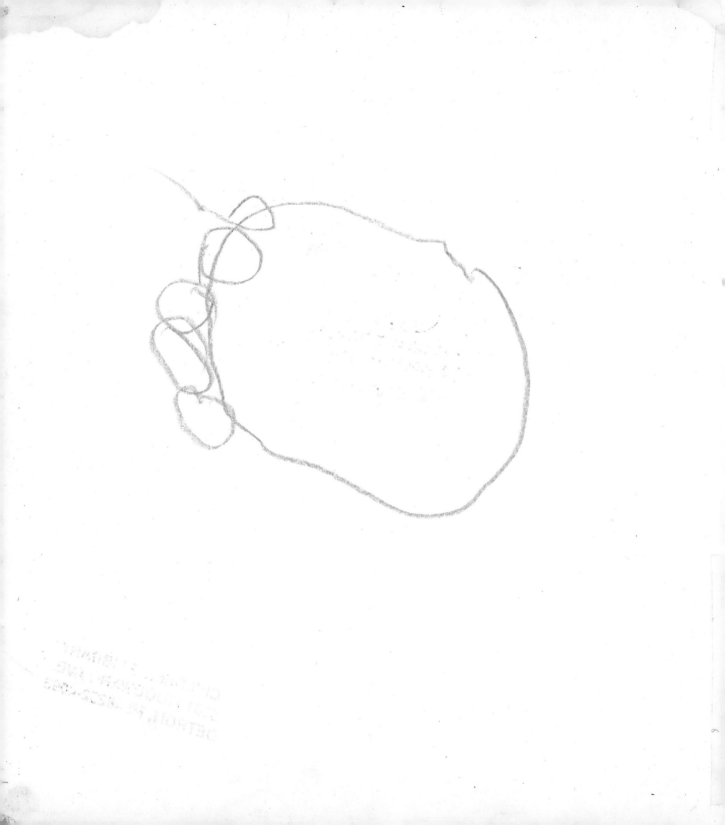

Tigers

Patricia Kendell

RAINTREE
STECK-VAUGHN
PUBLISHERS

A Harcourt Company

Austin   New York
www.raintreesteckvaughn.com

Chimpanzees Dolphins Elephants
Lions Polar Bears Tigers

Published by Raintree Steck-Vaughn Publishers,
an imprint of Steck-Vaughn Company

Library of Congress Cataloging-in-Publication Data

Kendell, Patricia.
  Tigers / Patricia Kendell.
    p. cm.—(In the wild)
  Includes bibliographical references (p.).
  Summary: An introduction to the physical characteristics, behavior, habitat, life cycle, and relationship with humans of this endangered animal.
  Includes bibliographical references (p.).
  ISBN 0-7398-4909-3
  1. Tiger—Juvenile literature. [1. Tiger. 2. Endangered species.]
  I. Title.II. Series.

QL737.C23 K47 2002
599.756—dc21   2002017826

Printed in Italy. Bound in the United States.

1 2 3 4 5 6 7 8 9 0 LB 07 06 05 04 03 02

Photograph acknowledgments:
Bruce Coleman 3 (fourth), 19, 29 (Rod Williams); FLPA 20 (T & P Gardner), 17, 21, 28 (David Hosking), 16 (E & D Hosking), 6 8, 13, 32 (Gerard Lacz), 15 (Silvestris), 3 (second), 1, 9 (T Whittaker), 5 (K Wothe); NHPA 26 (Martin Harvey), 3 (third), 7, 10 (Gerard Lacz), 4 (Andy Rouse); Oxford Scientific Films 11 (Zig Leszczynski), 18 (Vivek Sinha), 14, 27 (Belinda Wright); Stl Pictures 12 (J J Alcalay), 23 (Oliver Gillie), 22 (Michael Gunther), 25 (Alain Pons); Wayland Picture Library 24 (Jimmy Holmes).

Contents

Where Tigers Live

Tigers live in many different parts of Asia.
There are very few tigers left in the world.
More than half of those left live in India.

A few tigers live in the cold land of Siberia in Russia.

Baby Tigers

Baby tigers are called cubs. Cubs are blind and helpless when they are born in a **den**. After two months, these cubs are big enough to leave the den.

The cubs drink milk from their mother. As they grow,
the **tigress** will kill animals for them to eat.

Looking After the Cubs

If a tigress senses that her cubs are in danger, she will move them to another den. This tigress is carrying a cub gently in her mouth.

The tigress has to leave her cubs to hunt for food.
When she returns, she cuddles and licks the cubs
to let them know that they are safe.

Growing Up

Out of the den, the cubs stay near their mother.
She teaches them how to hunt, find water, and
keep out of danger.

The cubs play games with one another. They
pretend to fight and this helps them to grow strong.

Leaving Home

When the cubs are two years old, they leave their mothers to find a **territory** of their own.

Male tigers will fight over the best hunting territory.
They will also fight over female tigers.

Hunting

Tigers will hunt and kill animals such as large deer and **wild boar**. Sometimes tigers may hunt birds and other small animals. These deer are in danger of attack.

Tigers usually hunt alone. They creep toward their **prey** silently, and then pounce.

Out of Sight

When tigers are hunting, their stripes help them
to stay hidden in the tall grass.

Some animals, like these monkeys high in the trees, are safe. They spot the tigers moving through the grass and stay out of reach.

Eating and Drinking

Adult tigers will eat a big meal once or twice a week.

Tigers that live in hot places need to drink a lot to keep cool. Unlike most cats, they enjoy being in the water.

Resting

Tigers spend a lot of time sleeping, especially after a big meal. This tiger is ready for a nap.

While they rest, tigers **groom** themselves.

21

Dangers

Tigers are killed because people think that medicines made from tigers' bones have special healing powers.

People also sell tiger skin and make necklaces from tigers' teeth and claws.

Threats

People are taking more of the tigers' territory
to grow food and keep animals.

A hungry tiger will kill farmers' animals. But if this tiger steals an animal, the angry farmer might trap or poison him.

Protecting Tigers

These children in India are learning how to look after the places where tigers live.

This **orphan** tiger cub will be taken to a **protected area** where it will be safe.

Helping Tigers to Survive

Tourists pay to come and see tigers in these protected areas.

Local people use tourists' money to look after
the places where tigers live. The future looks
better for tigers in these areas.

Further Information

Find out more about how we can help tigers in the future.

ORGANIZATIONS TO CONTACT

Earth Living Foundation
P.O. Box 188
Hesperus, CO 81326
Tel: (970) 385-5500

Friends of the Earth
1025 Vermont Ave. N.W.
Suite 300
Washington, D.C. 20005-6303
Tel: (202) 783-7400

World Wildlife Fund
1250 24th Street, N.W.
Washington, D.C. 20037
Tel: (202) 293-4800

BOOKS

Butterfield, Moira. *What Am I?: Fast, Strong, and Striped*. New York: Raintree Steck-Vaughn, 1998.

Cowcher, Helen. *Tigress*. New York: Farrar Straus & Giroux, 1991.

Parsons, Alexandra. *Amazing Cats (Eyewitness Juniors)*. New York: Alfred A. Knopf, 1990.

Glossary

WEBSITES

Most young children will need adult help when visiting websites. Those listed have child-friendly pages that could be bookmarked.

Care for the Wild's site
www.careforthewild.org/education.asp
Meet an orphaned tiger from Laos, or enter a contest.

National Geographic site
www.nationalgeographic.com/kids/
This website explores conservation issues, and gives children's activities.

The Tiger Information Center
www.5tigers.org
Learn all about tigers and their conservation, including virtual adventures and teacher pages.

WWF's Endangered Species site
www.worldwildlife.org/species/
This website offers children fun activities, like making their own paper tiger.

den – a wild animal's home.

groom – to clean. Tigers do this by licking themselves.

orphan – (OR-fun) a young animal whose parents have died.

prey – an animal hunted by another animal for food.

protected area – (pruh-TEKT-ed AIR-ee-uh) safe places where wild animals can live freely.

territory – (TER-uh-tor-ee) the home area of an animal.

tigress – (TYE-griss) a female lion.

wild boar – a wild pig.

Index